How to Draw **MONSTERS** FOR KIDS

How to Draw
MONSTERS

FOR KIDS   A STEP-BY-STEP GUIDE

Ages 6–9

ROCKRIDGE
PRESS

Interior and Cover Designer: Francesca Pacchini
Art Producer: Sue Bischofberger
Editor: Alyson Penn
Production Editor: Ruth Sakata Corley

Illustration © 2021 Collaborate Agency
ISBN: Print 978-1-64876-634-3

R0

Part 1

Welcome to Drawing

Welcome to the wonderful world of drawing. Drawing can be a lot of fun, and inside this book you will find all the tools you need to get started.

Everyone can draw, but there's a catch. Ask any artist the secret to their success, and without fail, they will all tell you the same thing: practice, practice, practice. The fact is, the more you do something—anything—the better you will become. If you keep trying, you will be able to draw in a way you never dreamed possible.

Drawing is really important, and not just for the reasons you might think. Drawing can help you write, tell stories, share ideas, solve problems, build imagination, and relax after a stressful day. It can even make it easier to remember things!

So many things—from the movies you watch to the clothing you wear—began with a drawing. Now it's your turn to dive into drawing, because you never know where your first pencil marks will take you.

How to Use This Book

Alien

SECTIONS OF THE BOOK

In the first section, you will learn how to use this book and the basics of drawing, including shapes, form, and lines! The next section, "One-Page Drawings," is full of drawings, each broken down into six different steps. Look for the red lines to find out where to go next. Some of the red lines are guidelines that should be erased once your drawing is complete. That is very common in drawing!

The following section, "Two-Page Drawings," includes two illustrations that require 10 to 12 steps each to create. Because the finished products are a little more complex than the one-page drawings, they need a few more steps. Take your time, and have fun.

To strengthen your drawing skills, trace some of your favorite characters in the "Try Tracing" section (page 42). This will help you get a feel for how all of the lines and shapes fit together to create a finished work of art.

At the end of the book, you'll get creative! In "Decorated Scenes," you can use the backdrops as a stage for the characters you have learned to draw. Illustrate the drawings the way they look in the book, or draw them the way you want them to look—do whatever you want!

On the very last page, there are drawing prompts to encourage you to grab a pencil and paper and continue your new artistic journey.

Oni

 # MATERIALS

Before you draw, you will need to gather a few supplies. Pencils, paper, a pencil sharpener, and an eraser are the materials you will need to get started, along with some colored pencils (or crayons) for adding a pop of color.

To begin, use whatever paper you have available. But keep in mind, if you want to work with markers, pens, or paint, you will need thicker paper so your marks don't bleed through. Sketch pads are nice because all your drawings will be together in one place. Graph paper can be helpful for breaking your drawings down into small sections. Thin paper is great for tracing.

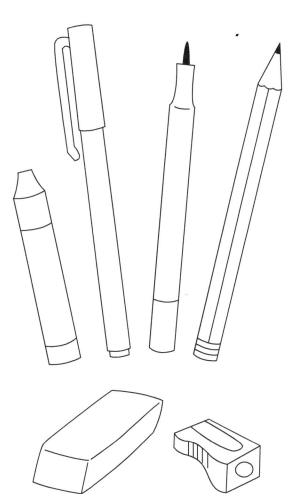

2 STEP-BY-STEP DRAWING METHOD

Looking at a blank piece of paper can feel really scary. It might even make you say, "I can't draw!" However, when you know exactly where to start, drawing becomes a whole lot easier.

We do most things in life one step at a time. We read books one page at a time, we play games one level at a time, and we build with blocks one piece at a time. Yet, when it comes to drawing, we think we should be able to produce a picture without first breaking it down into manageable chunks.

With a step-by-step drawing method, one line or shape creates a base for the next mark. So instead of feeling overwhelmed, you will have the confidence to make your first mark.

Chupacabra

③ MAKE IT YOUR OWN

Things are about to get interesting, because now you can start to use some of the skills you've already learned to create drawings of your favorite things.

Now that you know that even the most complicated drawings start out with just a few simple lines, you can take any image and break it down into smaller pieces. Begin with a shape, add a line, draw some more shapes, keep adding lines, and so on, until you have a finished work of art.

As soon as you train your eye to find the tiny pieces that make up the whole, you will be well on your way to becoming a line and shape detective who can draw anything. The possibilities are endless, because even the most complicated drawings start out with just one single line.

And remember, if at first you don't succeed, try, try again!

LEARNING TO DRAW

SHAPES

Shapes are flat, enclosed areas with length and width that are created by lines, shaded edges, or changes in color. They can be geometric, with hard sides like a square, circle, and triangle; or they can be organic, with irregular sides like clouds, flowers, and other natural shapes.

If you want to draw something—whether it's an animal, a car, a building, or a monster—you need to first look for the smaller shapes that make up the bigger picture. Once you start doing this, you won't be able to stop. Soon you will begin to see shapes everywhere you look.

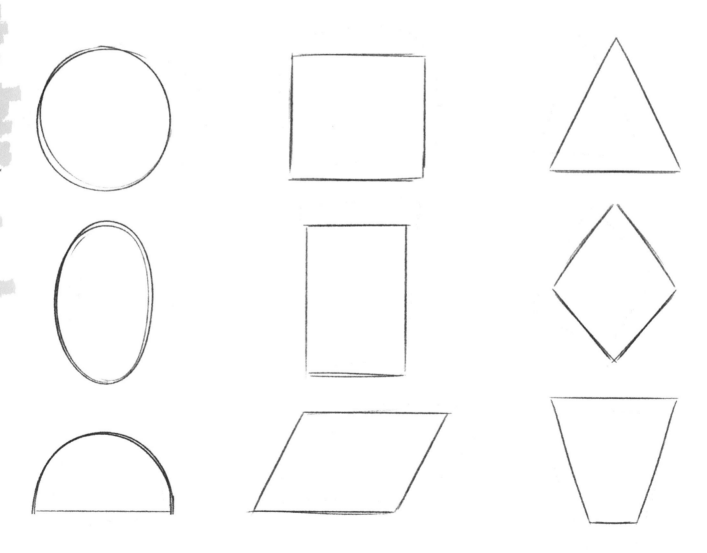

LINES

You can't make a drawing without lines, which is why artists love to use them. When looking at drawings, you will notice that lines can be thick or thin, long or short, straight or curvy. They are used to make shapes, create texture, and show feelings.

Horizontal lines run side to side, vertical lines run up and down, and contour lines run along the outside of a shape. In this book, guidelines are used to build the drawings, but they are designed to be erased. This is why it is really important to work lightly and not press too hard with your pencil.

Minotaur

Dragon

SPACE

You are a three-dimensional being, surrounded by space. Drawings, on the other hand, are flat and don't have space. However, you can create the illusion of space on a flat piece of paper by using a few creative tricks.

Overlapping objects in a drawing can create space and make something look like it's farther away than it actually is. The same effect can be created by making items different sizes. For example, a small tree drawn in the background will look like it is farther away from the viewer than a large tree in the foreground.

Fun fact: The area around an object is known as negative space.

FORM

You've learned that shapes are flat and have length and width. Form adds depth to shapes and is used in a drawing to make something appear three-dimensional, as though it could jump off the page.

Sculptures and other three-dimensional objects have form naturally, but to create the illusion of form (or depth) on a flat piece of paper, we need to get creative. We can use an imaginary light source, combined with shading techniques, to create the illusion of form in a drawing. Line variations, changes in color, and other visual tricks can also help to make something appear three-dimensional.

BALANCE

Balance in a drawing refers to how the objects on the page are placed and whether or not the picture looks symmetrical (meaning both sides are even, or the same) or asymmetrical (meaning the sides are uneven, or different). People generally like looking at things that are symmetrical because they feel balanced and comfortable. But if you want to create drama in a drawing, make sure you add a few things to make your picture look a little off-center or unbalanced.

Werewolf

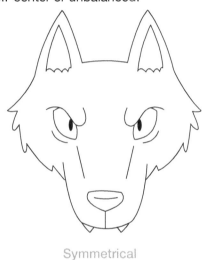

Symmetrical

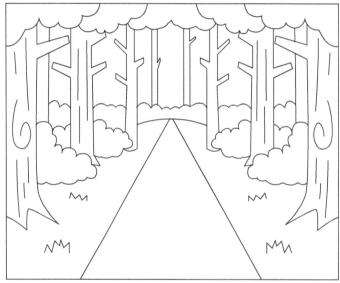

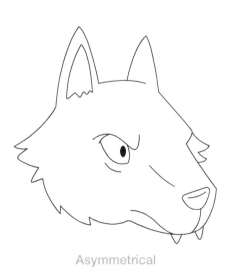

Asymmetrical

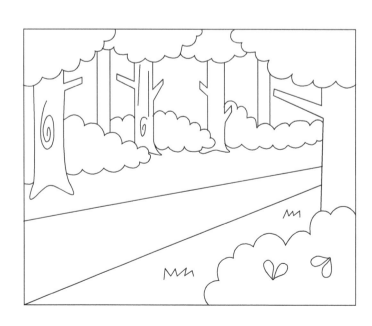

One-Page Drawings

Here is where the guided drawings begin. Remember, these six-step drawings have been created so you can see how each line and shape builds on the previous line or shape. Look for the red lines to lead you through each drawing.

GHOST

ALIEN

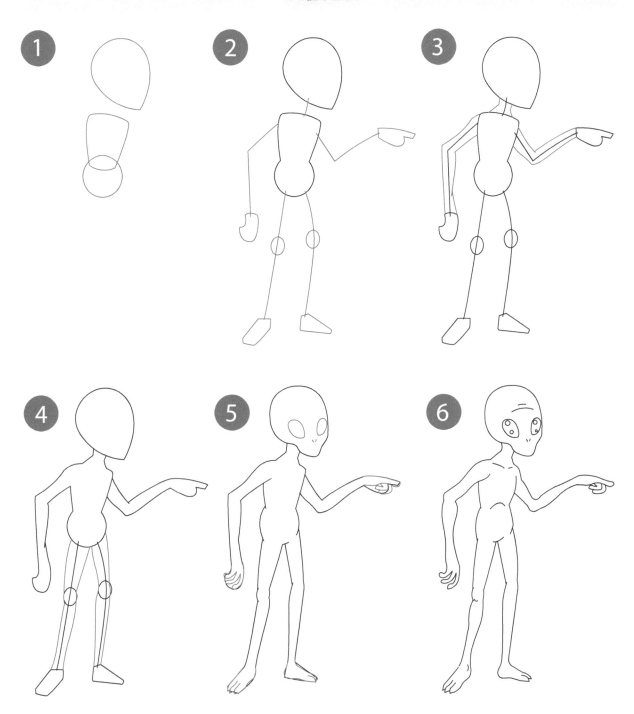

LOCH NESS MONSTER

1

2

3

4

5

6

TROLL

YETI

The yeti is similar to the Sasquatch (or Bigfoot) of North America.

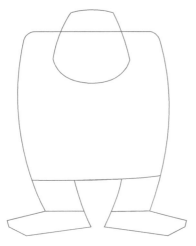

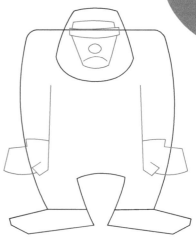

BANSHEE

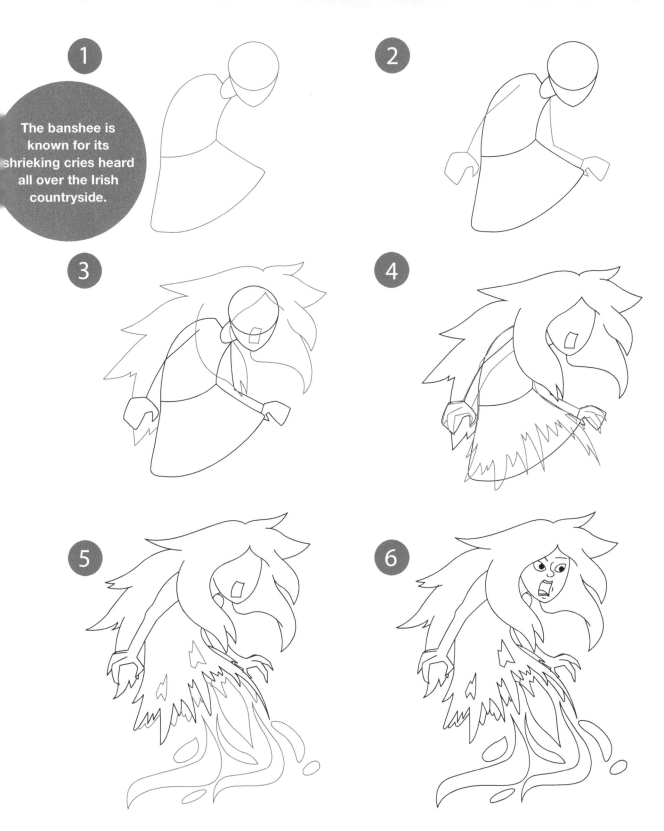

The banshee is known for its shrieking cries heard all over the Irish countryside.

CYCLOPS

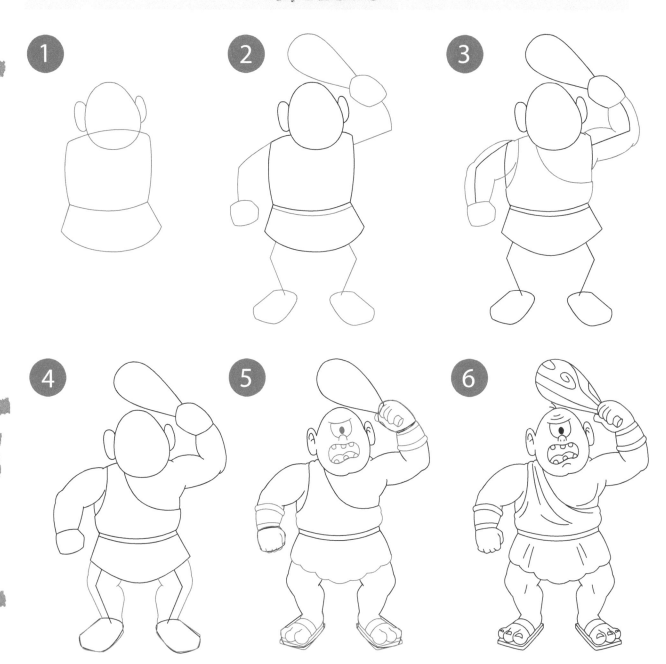

MUMMY

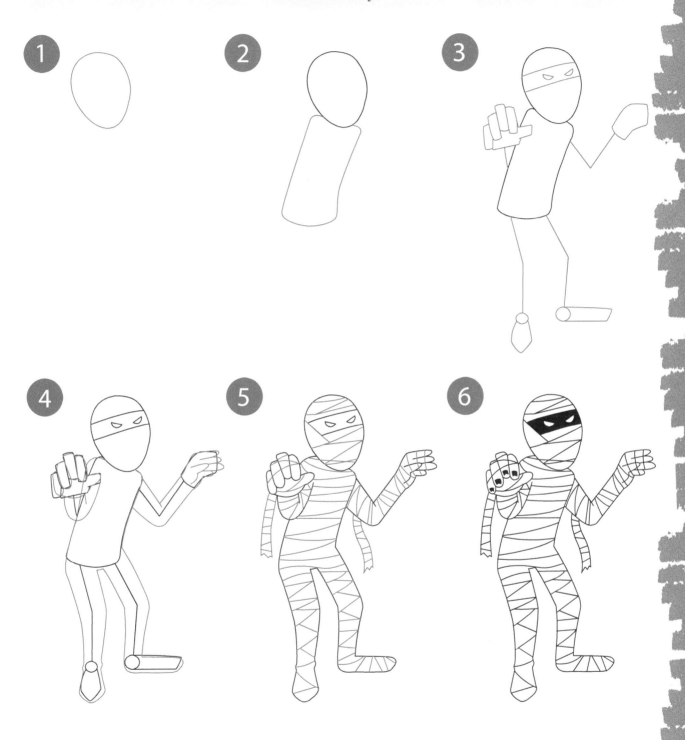

VAMPIRE

WEREWOLF

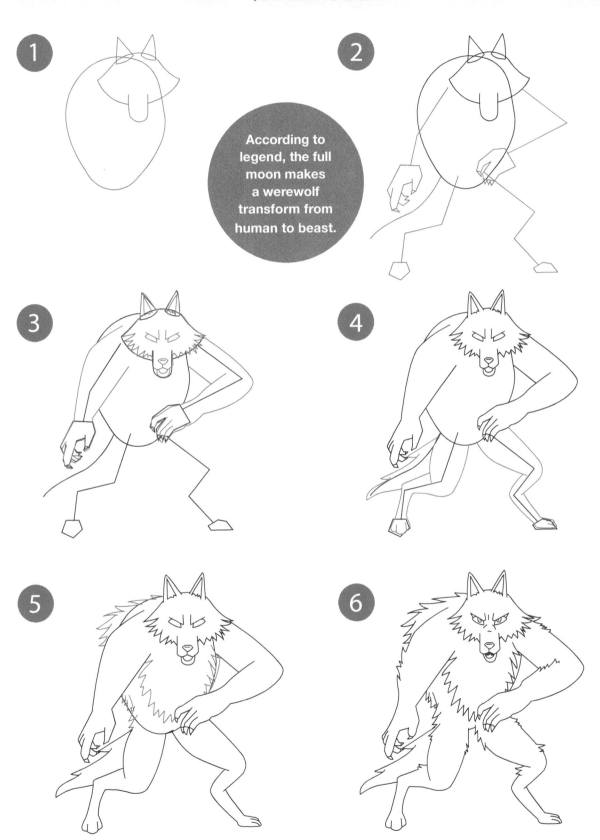

According to legend, the full moon makes a werewolf transform from human to beast.

KAPPA

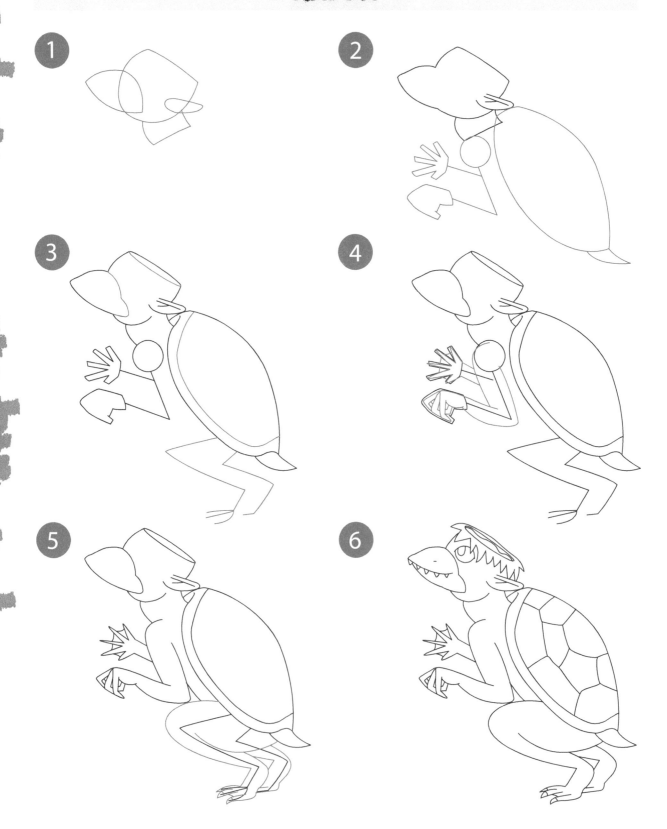

GOBLIN

CHUPACABRA

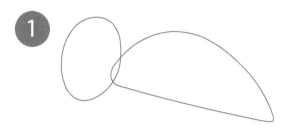

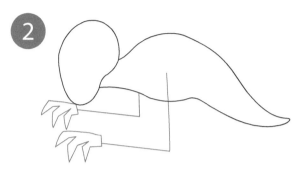

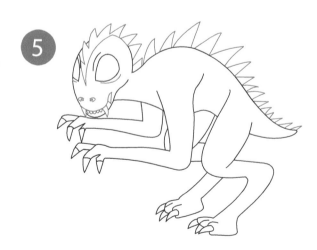

ZOMBIE

AMMIT

GORGON

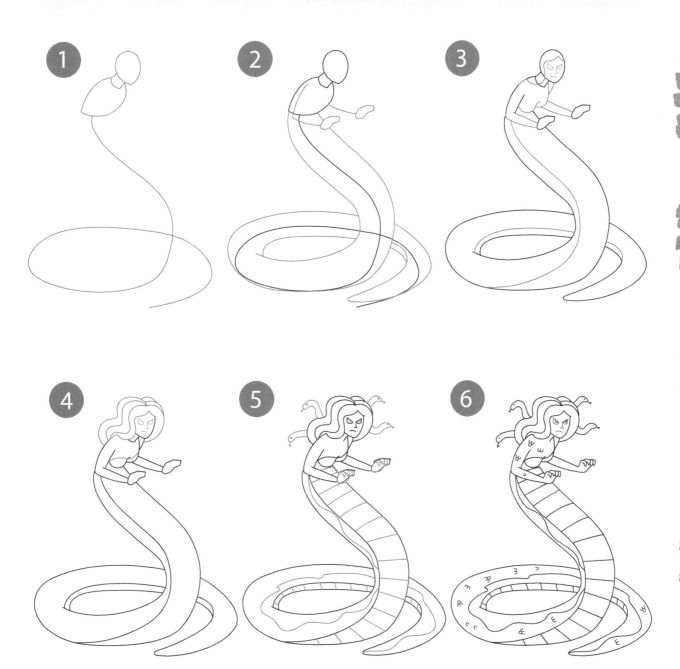

LESHY

 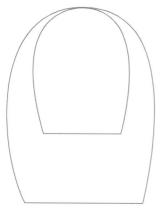

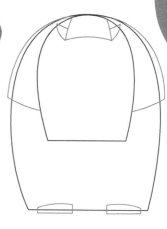

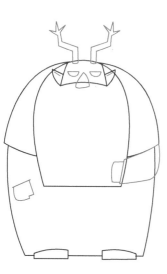 

KRAKEN

The kraken is large enough to destroy whole ships with its tentacles.

DRAGON

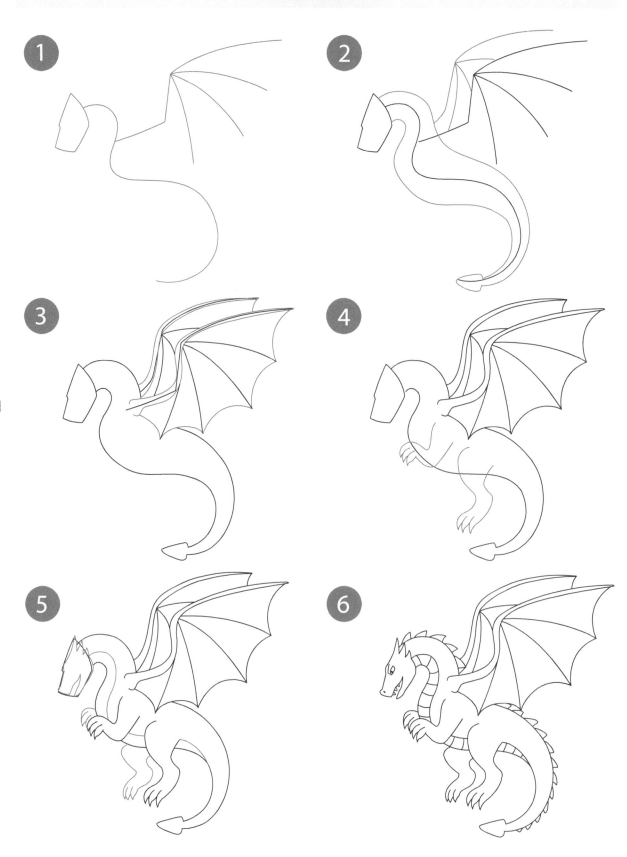

BASILISK

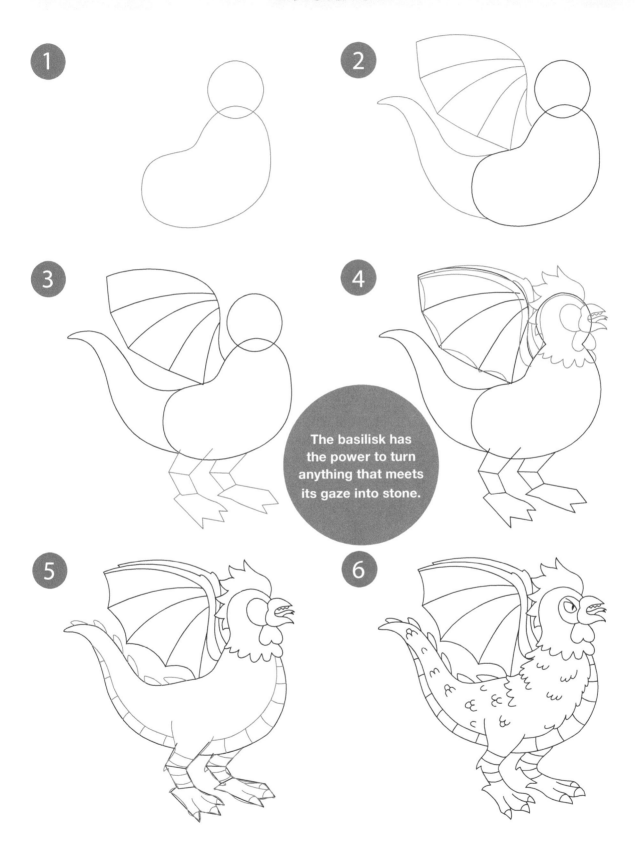

The basilisk has the power to turn anything that meets its gaze into stone.

MINOTAUR

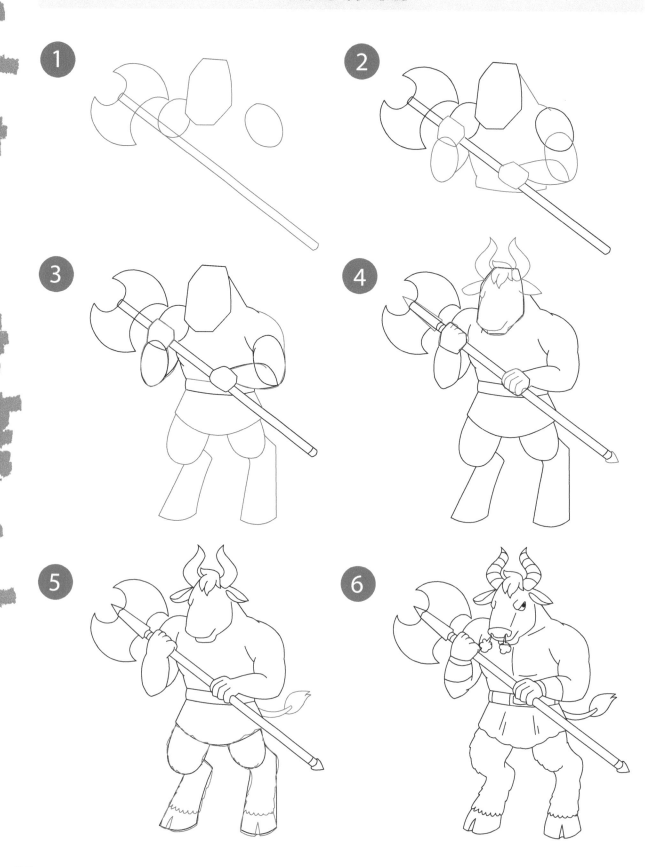

CERBERUS

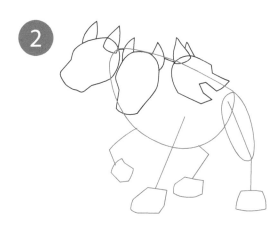

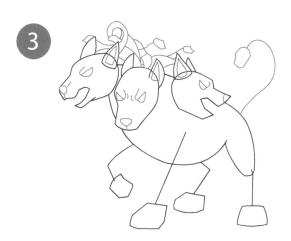

SPHINX

ONI

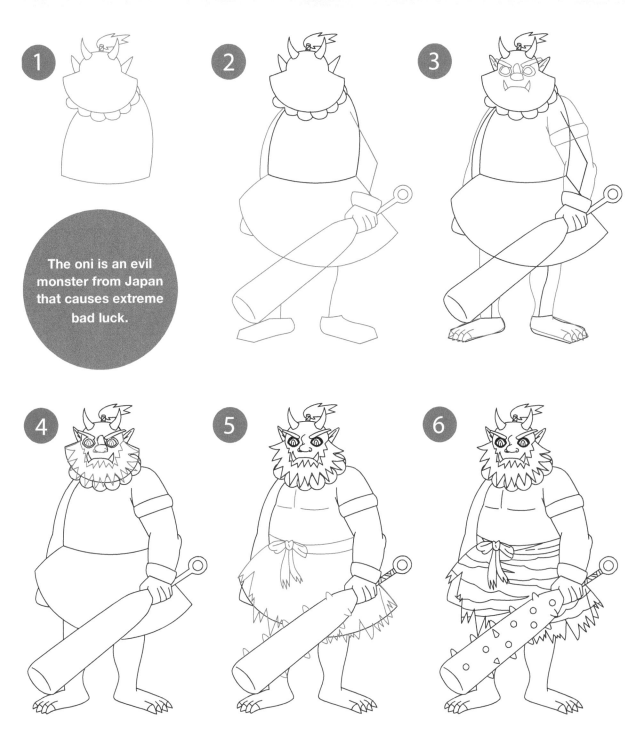

The oni is an evil monster from Japan that causes extreme bad luck.

MANTICORE

The manticore is part human, part lion, and part scorpion.

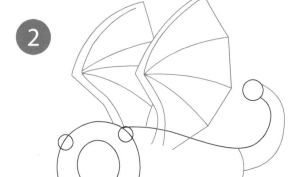

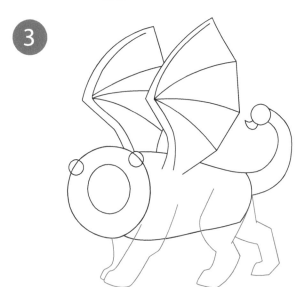

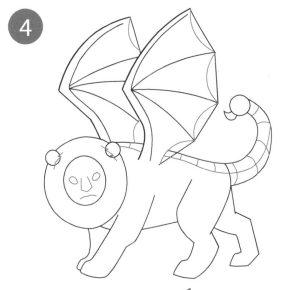

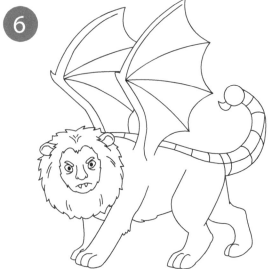

Two-Page Drawings

These drawings require a few more steps than the drawings you've already done, but that doesn't mean they are more difficult. Use the skills you learned while doing the one-step drawings. Don't forget to work lightly so you can erase your guidelines once your drawings are complete. At the end, trace some of your favorite creatures to strengthen your drawing skills.

ANANSI

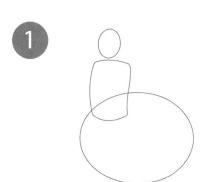 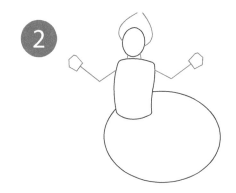

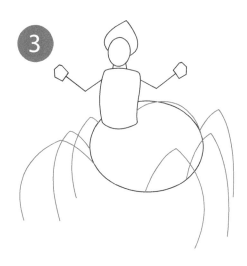 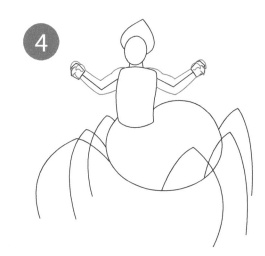

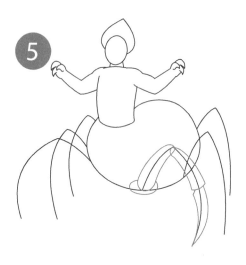 

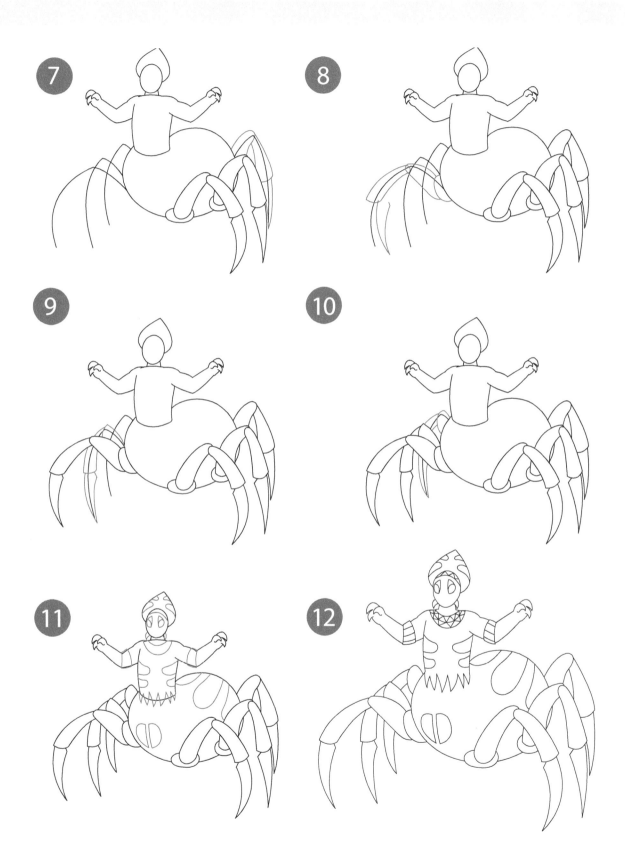

CHIMERA

The first Chimera was defeated by another mythical beast: Pegasus, the flying horse!

TRY TRACING

Trace these monsters to practice your skills.

Part 4

Creative Exploration

Now it's time to get creative! You have mastered the skill of drawing step-by-step, and you've practiced by tracing your new creations. In this section, you can use the fun backgrounds to stage all your creatures in different settings. At the very end, grab a pencil and paper and draw scenes from your imagination.

DECORATED SCENES

Draw your favorite monsters in these different scenes!

TROPICAL BEACH

ENCHANTED FOREST

SPOOKY GRAVEYARD

HAUNTED MANSION

NOW IT'S YOUR TURN

Use your imagination! Grab a piece of paper and draw the following prompts.

→ Draw a werewolf and vampire dancing in outer space.

→ Draw a kraken stealing gold from a pirate ship.

→ Draw Anansi and a yeti sharing secrets in a tree house.

→ Draw a mummy playing fetch with Cerberus.

→ Draw the Leshy standing in a field full of mushrooms.

→ Draw a goblin lighting a birthday cake with a torch.

→ Draw a dragon exploring a cave filled with magical crystals.

→ Draw a kappa having a tea party with a zombie.

→ Draw a Gorgon roasting marshmallows with a banshee.

→ Draw the Loch Ness Monster blowing bubbles with an underwater ghost.